P9-CQJ-486

0 00 30 0316833 7

The 3-D Library of the Human Body

THE EAR
LEARNING HOW WE HEAR

Josepha Sherman

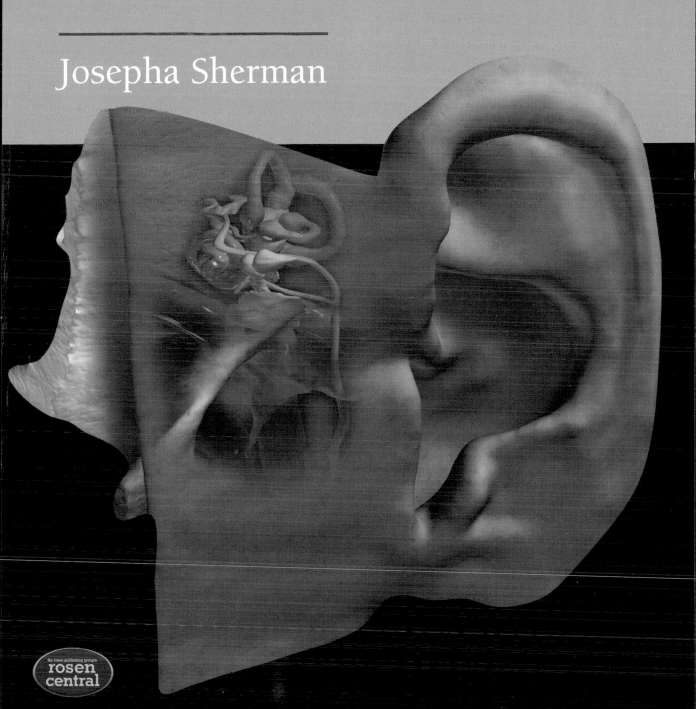

the rosen publishing group's
rosen central

Editor's Note

The idea for the illustrations in this book originated in 1986 with the Vesalius Project at Colorado State University's Department of Anatomy and Neurobiology. There, a team of scientists and illustrators dreamed of turning conventional two-dimensional anatomical illustrations into three-dimensional computer images that could be rotated and viewed from any angle, for the benefit of students of medicine and biology. In 1988 this dream became the Visible Human Project™, under the sponsorship of the National Library of Medicine in Bethesda, Maryland. A grant was awarded to the University of Colorado School of Medicine, and in 1993 the first work of dissection and scanning began on the body of a Texas convict who had been executed by lethal injection. The process was repeated on the body of a Maryland woman who had died of a heart attack. Applying the latest techniques of computer graphics, the scientific team was able to create a series of three-dimensional digital images of the human body so beautiful and startlingly accurate that they seem more in the realm of art than science. On the computer screen, muscles, bones, and organs of the body can be turned and viewed from any angle, and layers of tissue can be electronically peeled away to reveal what lies underneath. In reproducing these digital images in two-dimensional print form, the editors at Rosen have tried to preserve the three-dimensional character of the work by showing organs of the body from different perspectives and using illustrations that progressively reveal deeper layers of anatomical structure.

Published in 2002 by The Rosen Publishing Group, Inc.
29 East 21st Street, New York, NY 10010

Copyright © 2002 by The Rosen Publishing Group, Inc.

All digital anatomy images copyright © 1999 by Visible Productions.

Digital anatomy images published by arrangement with Anatographica, LLC.
216 East 49th Street, New York, NY 10017

First Edition

Library of Congress Cataloging-in-Publication Data

Sherman, Josepha.
The ear: learning how we hear / Josepha Sherman. — 1st ed.
p. cm. — (The 3-D library of the human body)
Summary: Discusses the anatomy and functions of the human ear.
ISBN 0-8239-3529-9
1. Ear—Juvenile literature. 2. Hearing—Juvenile literature. [1. Ear. 2. Hearing. 3. Senses and sensation.]
I. Title. II. Series.
QP462.2 .S54 2001
612.8'5—dc21

2001002574

Manufactured in the United States of America

CONTENTS

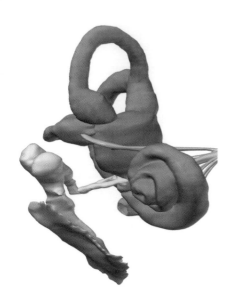

PREFACE
THOMAS
SYDENHAM

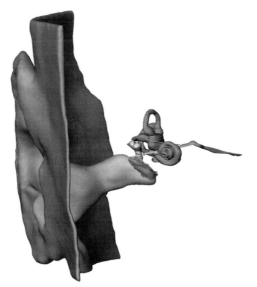

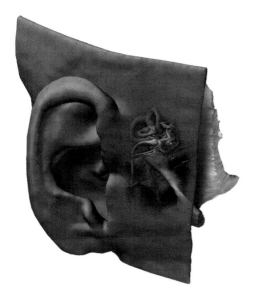

English physician Thomas Sydenham (1624–1689) was one of the most important radical medical reformers of the seventeenth century. Because of his politics, his influence during his lifetime was not great. Eventually, however, he came to be known as the English Hippocrates.

Sydenham was born into a family of wealthy gentry, but he sided with Oliver Cromwell and against King Charles I in the English Civil War (1642–1651). Cromwell's supporters wanted to reduce the power of the English king and increase the power of the English Parliament. Sydenham became a captain in the parliamentary army and fought in several fierce battles. His military career interrupted his education. He did not get his master's degree until 1648, and he did not begin practicing medicine until 1656.

It was in fact his inability to advance himself in public life that made Sydenham turn to medicine. After the defeat of Cromwell and the restoration of King Charles II, there was no room in politics or society for people with antimonarchist views. So Sydenham set up a practice in London and applied his reformer's passion to medical science. Sydenham agreed with the ancient Greek physician Hippocrates (460–377 BC) that observation and experience counted for more than theory. He insisted upon the need to observe patients and their symptoms carefully and to keep detailed case histories.

The result of all this careful observation and recording of symptoms was the publication of *Medical Observations*, in which Sydenham described precisely the effects of diseases he had studied in London from 1661 to 1675. This was the first accurate description of such diseases as measles, dysentery, gout, and cholera. By carefully discriminating between symptoms, Sydenham was able to identify a new disease, scarlet fever. Unfortunately, Sydenham also adopted Hippocrates' belief that diseases were caused by imbalances in the four "humours": blood, phlegm, black bile, and yellow bile. At the time of Hippocrates, such a theory was an advance over the ancient notion that the gods caused illnesses because it advanced the idea of natural causes for disease. Inaccurate though the theory was, it was all that Sydenham had to work with. The germ theory of disease would not be introduced until the nineteenth century. In spite of this, Sydenham is considered the founder of modern clinical medicine and epidemiology, the science of disease control in populations. His studies of epidemics would remain the best knowledge available to doctors until the work of Louis Pasteur (1822–1895).

Sydenham was also the first doctor to use laudanum, an opium derivative, to relieve pain. He promoted the use of cinchona bark, which contains quinine, to treat malaria. He used iron to treat patients suffering from anemia. He belonged to a small group of doctors and scientists who, even before the industrial and scientific revolutions of the eighteenth century, tried to turn medical science away from its dependence upon ancient authorities.

1
THE EAR

When we mention the human ear, we're usually referring only to the part that we can see: the outer ear from which we hang earrings or that we are reminded to clean behind. But there's a great deal more to the ear than what is easily visible.

The whole outer ear is called the auricle, which means "ear" in Latin. The bendable segment is the pinna, from the Latin word that means "leaf," because it looks something like a leaf. (You can see a clearer leaf shape in the ear of an animal like a dog or horse.) Latin, by the way, is the language often used in science. At one time it was the language that all scholars held in common, and every scientist understood it.

The auricle is made of a thin plate of cartilage tightly covered by skin. Cartilage is a form of connective tissue, more flexible and compressible than bone. The ear is attached to the side of the head by several small muscles, most of which serve no other use and have no strength, although the occasional person can wiggle his or her ears with them.

The curve of the outer ear, the portion of the ear farthest from the ear's attachment to the head, is known as the helix. This name comes to us through Latin from the Greek word for "curve" or "folding in." The edge of the outer curve is the crux of the helix, from

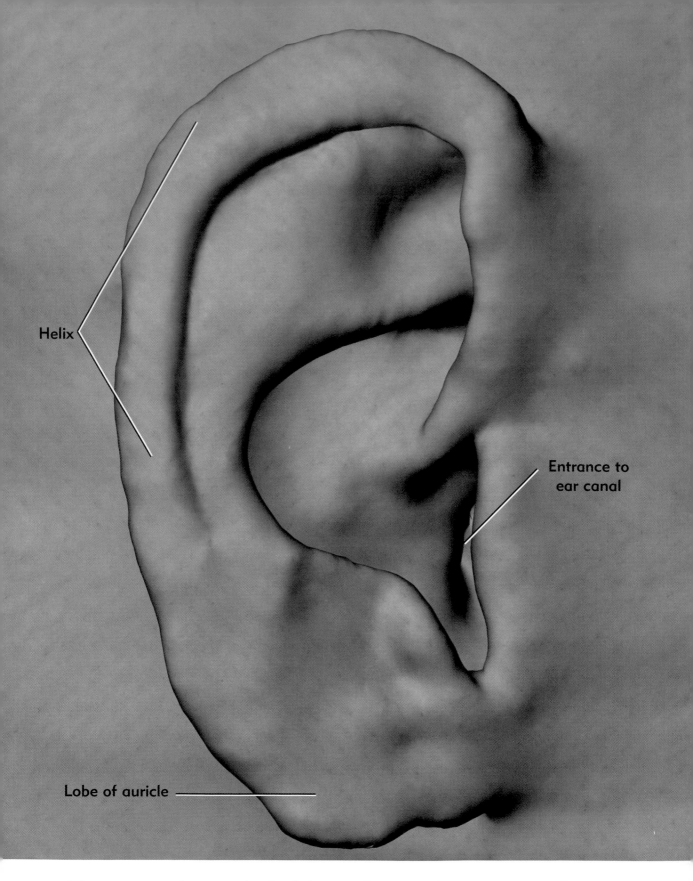

Helix

Entrance to
ear canal

Lobe of auricle

The outer ear is comprised of the ear flap and the entrance to the ear canal.

the Latin for "cross," meaning the main point of the helix. Follow the curve down to the bottom of the ear, and there is the fleshy lobule, more commonly known as the earlobe. Different people have different lengths and shapes to their earlobes, but there doesn't seem to be any scientific reason for the variations. The lobule plays no role in hearing.

Curving in from the helix at the top of the ear is what seems to be a true canal. But the indentation quickly ends in a small bowl. In fact, it barely seems to be worth being named a canal at all, but its scientific name is the helix canal. The lower side of the helix canal "bowl," which is lower than the crux of the helix, is named the anti-helix, meaning that it's an opposite of the true helix.

Below the antihelix are the concha and the cavum of concha. Concha is the Latin word for "shell," and that part of the ear really does look something like a shell. "Cavum" means exactly what it

Animal Ears

Humans rely more on sight than on hearing. But animals that depend on hearing to warn them of predators or alert them to prey have large, pointed ears that "cup" sound. Their ear muscles are better developed than those in humans, letting them turn their ears in all directions to locate a specific noise.

Animals with mobile ears also use them as part of their "language." A curious dog will prick his ears straight up, but he'll flatten his ears back if he's angry. And a bored or sleepy dog will just let his ears flop.

seems—this is the start of the "cave" of the ear canal. It has the more scientific name of the external auditory canal, or the external auditory meatus. "Meatus" is the Latin word for a natural opening.

This is as much as can be seen of the ear with the eye alone. But the external auditory canal continues inward for a little over an inch. The canal is lined all the way with fine hairs pointing outward and has modified sweat glands that produce cerumen, or earwax. Both are there to keep foreign objects, such as insects, out of the ear.

The auditory canal ends at the tympanic membrane. This is another name that should be easily understood by anyone who knows that the formal word for drums is tympani. The tympanic membrane is a thin strip of skin that looks like the head of a drum; in fact, its common name is the eardrum. Richly filled with nerve endings and tiny blood vessels, it's extremely sensitive to noise and pain, and can be relatively easily damaged. Many injuries to the eardrum will heal themselves without leaving a loss of hearing, but it's better to be careful. When cleaning out an ear, for instance, never use anything that might push earwax—or anything else—against the membrane.

Beyond the thin membrane of the eardrum lies the air-filled cavity of the middle ear and the loosely connected sections of the ossicular chain. The word "ossicular" is the Latin term for "bony." An ossicular chain is exactly what the middle ear holds: a linking of three tiny bones. All three get their names from their appearances. The first bone is the malleus, which is Latin for "hammer." The second bone is the incus, which is Latin for "anvil," and the third and farthest in from the middle ear is the stapes, which means the "stirrup." While you need a little imagination to see a hammer or an anvil in the first two bones, the stapes really does look the most like its namesake, down to the flat base of the stapes that looks very much like the base of an English saddle's stirrup.

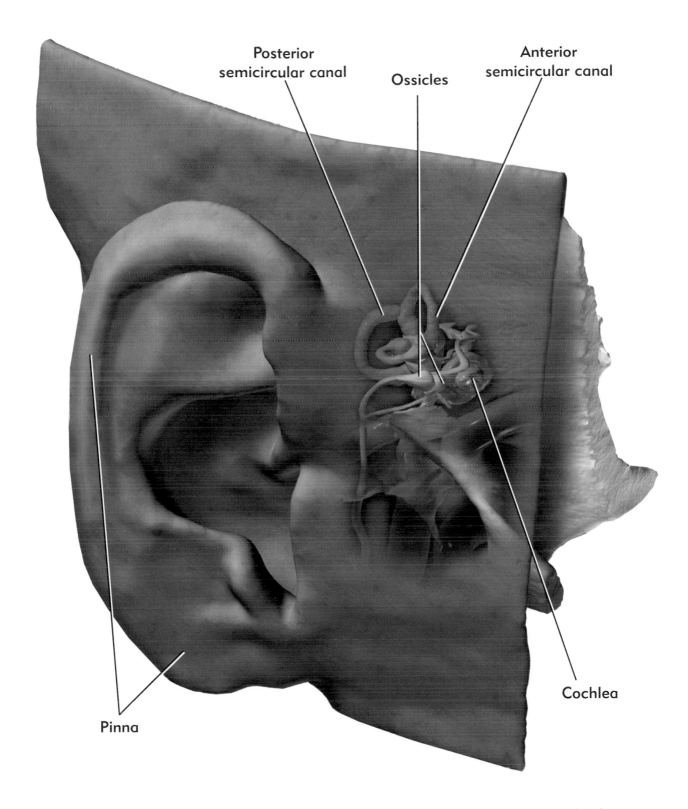

Posterior
semicircular canal

Ossicles

Anterior
semicircular canal

Cochlea

Pinna

This view of the head with part of the temporal bone removed reveals the components of the inner ear.

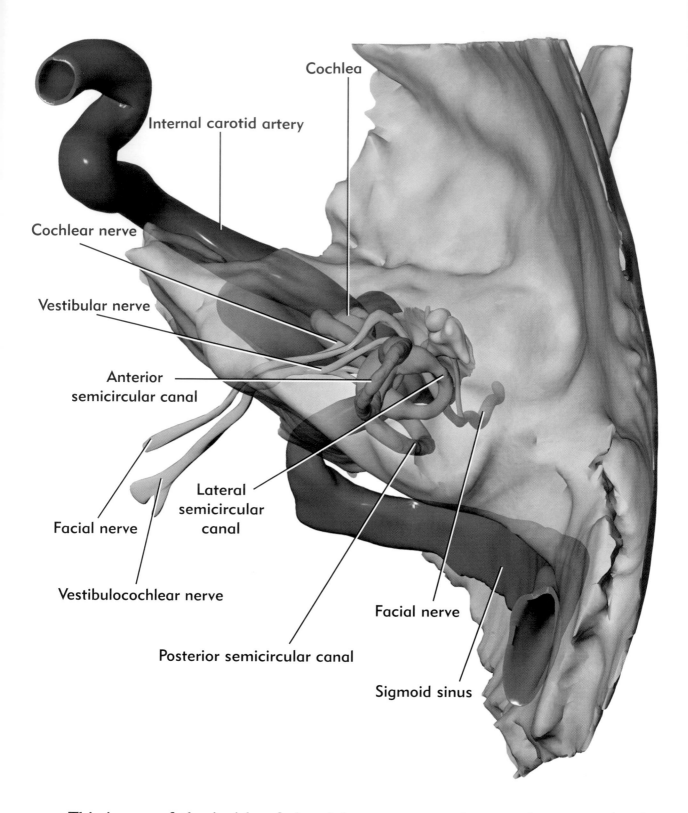

Cochlea

Internal carotid artery

Cochlear nerve

Vestibular nerve

Anterior
semicircular canal

Facial nerve

Lateral
semicircular
canal

Vestibulocochlear nerve

Facial nerve

Posterior semicircular canal

Sigmoid sinus

This image of the inside of the right ear exposes its complex network of canals and nerves.

Also found in the middle ear is one end of the eustachian tube, which is made up of bone and cartilage and lined with tiny hair cells called cilia. The other end of the eustachian tube is attached to the pharynx. This is the cavity at the back of the mouth that leads down into the esophagus, which is more commonly known as the

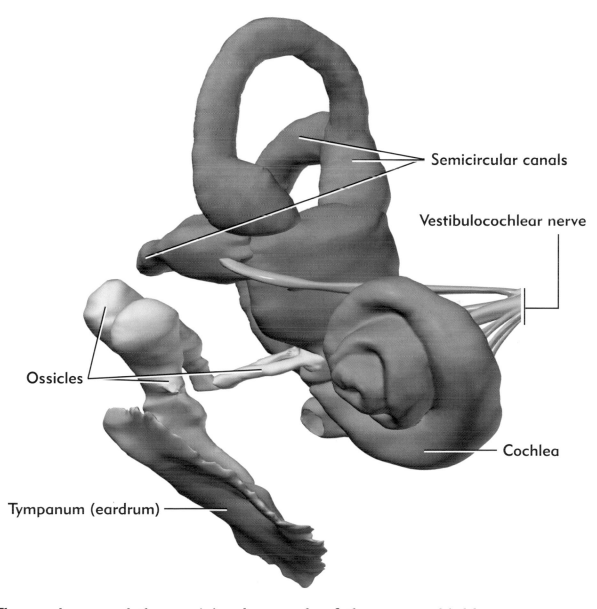

The eardrum and the semicircular canals of the ear are highly specialized structures.

windpipe, and which lets us breathe through our mouths as well as our noses. Not every mammal has this opening. The horse, for instance, does not have it, and, as a result, usually doesn't breathe through its mouth.

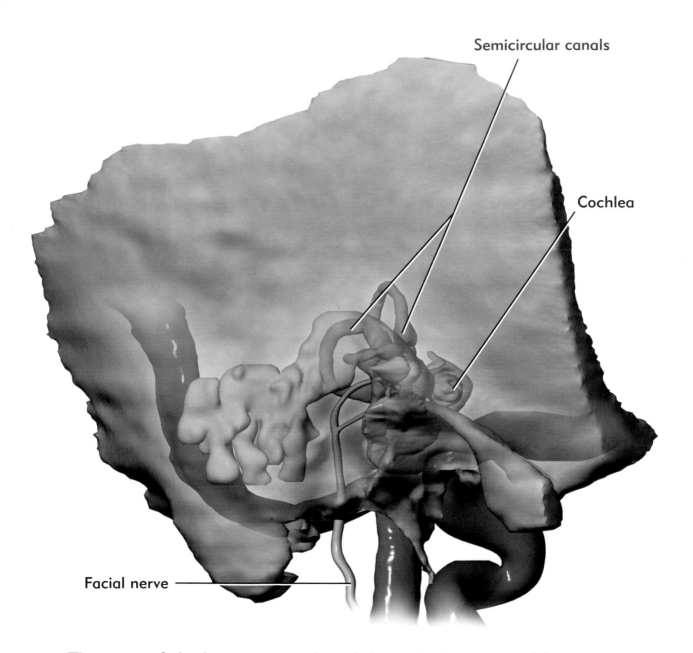

The parts of the inner ear as viewed through the temporal bone.

The eustachian tube lets fluid flow properly down the throat, and it keeps the pressure equal on both sides of the eardrum. It also allows excess fluid to drain out of the middle ear and opens wide to let air flow in or out of it three or four times during a yawn, a chew, or a swallow.

The base of the stapes rests against the main structure of the inner ear, the cochlea. This and the whole inner ear comprise a complex system of fluid-filled tubes and sacs that is called the bony labyrinth, and it really does look like one big maze.

But for all its complexity, the cochlea is tiny, no bigger than the very tip of a little finger. The word "cochlea" means "snail" in Latin, and that's roughly what it looks like: a snail facing toward the middle ear, but one with three looping tubes coming out of its head. About where the eye would be on the snail is the oval, or vestibular window, made of a thin, vibrating membrane. The three tubes that come up and loop down again to the cochlea are, starting with the one closest to the middle ear, the lateral semicircular canal, the posterior semicircular canal, and the anterior semicircular canal. They are filled with fluid and lined, like the eustachian tube, with cilia. What looks like the snail's body is the coiled-up cochlear nerve. Resting on what would be the snail's back is the vestibular nerve. This is a segment of the acoustic nerve, one of the eight cranial nerves of the brain.

2
HEARING AND BALANCE

It probably seems pretty obvious to everyone that the ear's primary function is to allow someone to hear. But what is not so obvious is that the ear actually has two functions. Not only does it let someone hear, the ear also allows that person to stand, turn, and walk. How the ear achieves all this is a process that's both amazingly complex and amazingly swift and accurate.

The process of hearing, of course, has to begin with a sound, such as the ringing of a phone. Sound is produced when an action, such as that telephone ringing, sets air molecules vibrating. The vibrations, in turn, become sound waves. As anyone who has ever swum underwater or listened to recordings of whale songs knows, sound waves can travel through air or water and still be heard. Though we can't see a sound wave, it is as real as an ocean wave, though it would look a little different. Instead of waving up and down, sound waves consist of regions of compressed, or tightly packed, air molecules, followed by regions where the air molecules are more thinly packed. The distance between two tightly packed regions is called the wavelength. The rate at which these tightly packed regions move past a fixed point is called the frequency. The molecules themselves don't change position much. The wave, or disturbance, that passes through the air molecules is energy.

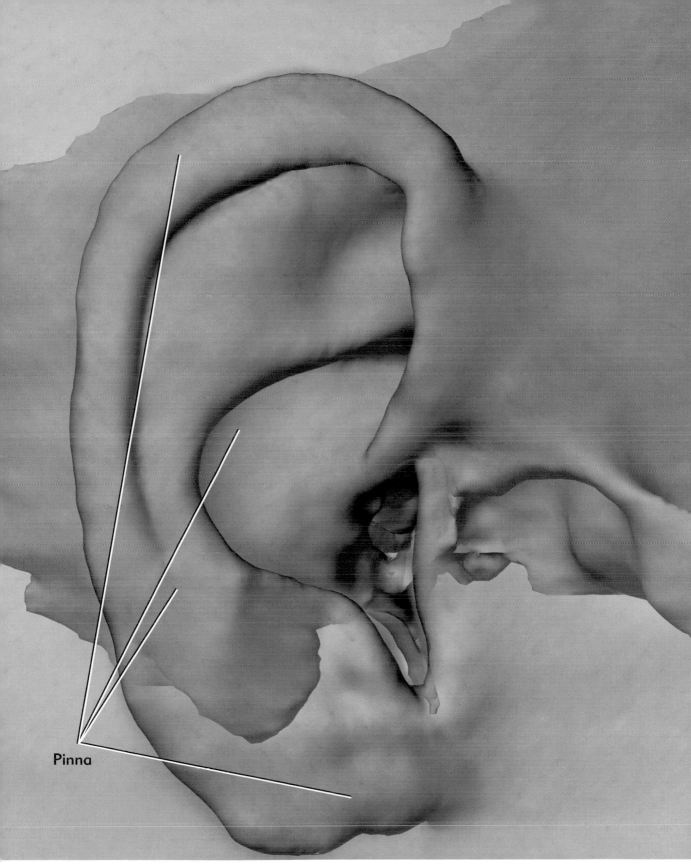

Pinna

Not only do the ears enable us to hear, they also provide us with balance, allowing us to stand, turn, and walk.

Sound and Speed

While sound can travel through both air and water, it cannot travel through a vacuum. Space is, of course, a vacuum. When moviemakers first started to film science fiction, they discovered something funny about the human ear and mind. We are conditioned to hear something move, especially something that's supposed to be whizzing by at great speed. We also expect an explosion to make a loud noise. Without sound, the excitement of a high-speed chase in outer space was missing, and the shock of an exploding planet just wasn't shocking enough. The moviemakers had to add sound effects to their movies to make spaceships roar across the screen and explosions really go "boom!"

The sound wave is caught and "cupped" by the curve of the outer ear, the external auricle, and funneled toward the ear canal, down which it travels until it reaches the tympanic membrane, the eardrum. The sound wave strikes the membrane and is transformed into vibrations in the eardrum. This is the same thing that happens when sound waves strike a microphone and cause its artificial membrane to vibrate.

But not all wave frequencies can make the human eardrum vibrate. We can't, for instance, hear sounds at too high a frequency because the sound waves travel one after another too swiftly to give the membrane a chance to vibrate. Those extremely fast frequencies are called ultrasonic. Some mammals, such as dogs and bats, have specialized ear structures and can hear them, but we cannot. The ear's perception of sound-wave frequency is called pitch: the greater the frequency, the higher the pitch.

Another factor in the proper transmission of the sound wave is its intensity. If it's too faint, or too soft, like a sound created by a whisper or from something far away, it barely causes a vibration of the eardrum. If it's too intense a sound wave, it causes genuine pain. We say that such painful sounds are too loud. We also can measure them in a scale using units of measurement called decibels. A jet engine at full throttle, for instance, will produce far more decibels, 130, than normal conversation, which produces 50 to 60 decibels. A rock concert, incidentally, produces about 100 decibels. The threshold of pain is at about 110 decibels.

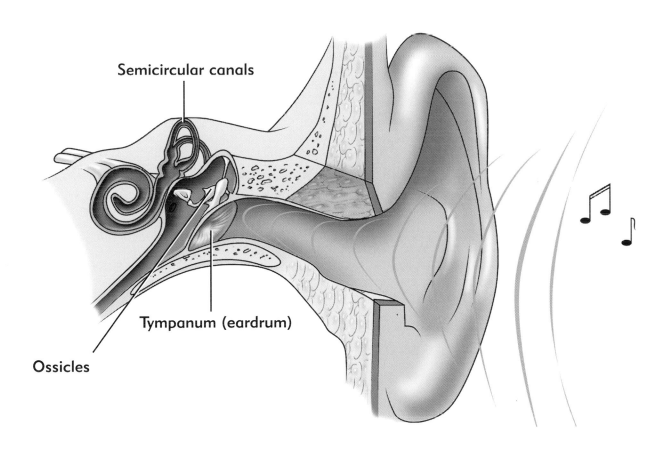

Semicircular canals

Tympanum (eardrum)

Ossicles

The outer ear collects and channels sound waves from the air through the ear canal and into the eardrum.

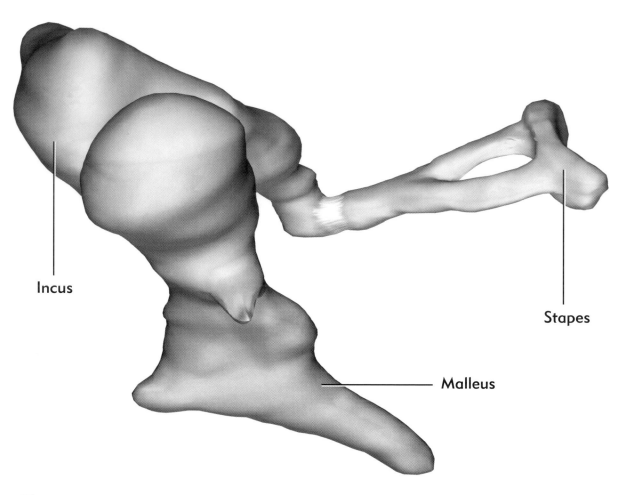

These are the bones of the inner ear. The eardrum sets these bones vibrating. These vibrations are detected by the organ of Corti in the cochlea and signals are then sent to the brain.

Those sound waves that are within the normal human range of hearing succeed in creating vibrations in the membrane that are passed inward to the middle ear. The vibrations strike the handle of the malleus, which is the first bone in the ossicular chain. The vibrations speed to the head of the malleus and from it to the incus. The vibrations are passed along to the stapes, which swings back and forth, passing them in turn to the oval window of the cochlea and the organ of Corti within the cochlea. Now the sound vibrations are transformed to liquid vibrations through the cochlea's

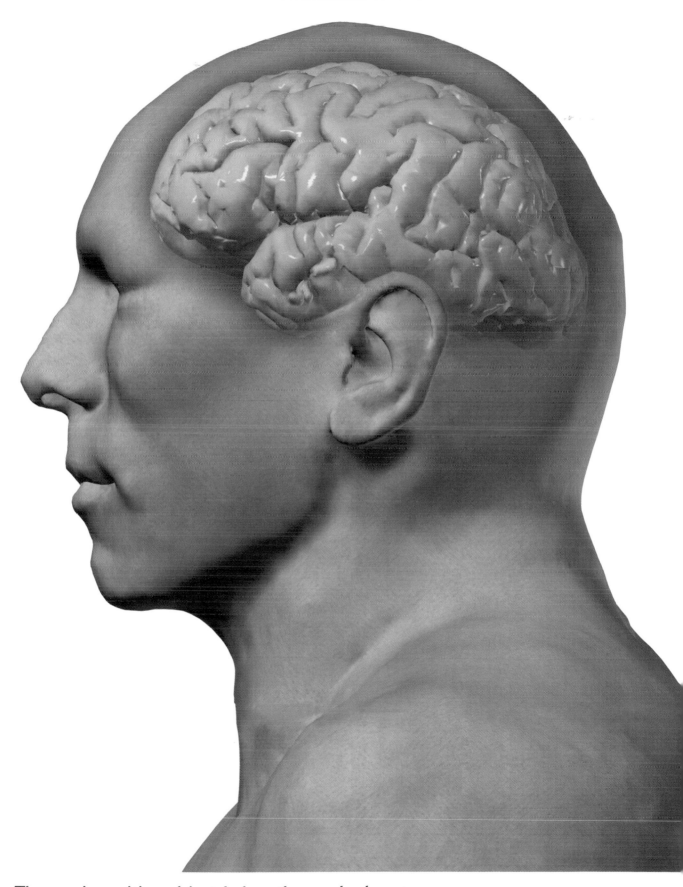

The ear is positioned just below the cerebral cortex.

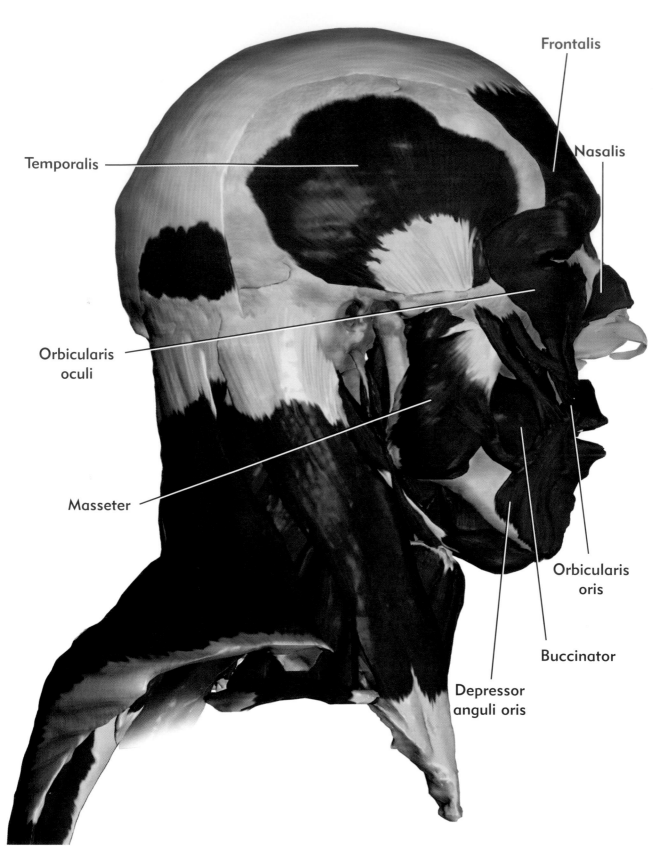

Frontalis

Nasalis

Temporalis

Orbicularis
oculi

Masseter

Orbicularis
oris

Buccinator

Depressor
anguli oris

Your face and neck are comprised of many muscles that help you talk,
eat, and smile.

fluid. They are analyzed, sorted, and transformed again, this time into neural impulses that travel to the brain. The brain translates the sound as that of a ringing phone. What's more, the angle at which the sound waves strike the outer ear give the brain clues as to the telephone's location.

It's truly astonishing that so much analysis and translation takes place in far less time than a second. What's more, the ear and brain are constantly processing sounds at the same time and almost never make a mistake. The system isn't perfect, of course, since the brain can't identify something the ear hasn't heard before. We can get confused if the telephone sounds too much like the doorbell. But we don't make mistakes about the sounds that are important to us. The sound of a baby crying or a fire alarm clanging will create instant recognition.

Balance

For centuries, nobody knew that the structure of the ear was so complicated. But in the seventeenth century, scientists began making careful studies of the ear. They assumed, though, that the inner ear served only the function of hearing, and they weren't sure what part of that function the semicircular canals served. It wasn't until French scientist Marie Jean Pierre Flourens began working with pigeons in 1824 that he discovered that the ear is also responsible for giving us balance. It wasn't until the end of that century that his findings were internationally accepted. Science sometimes hears only what it wants to hear.

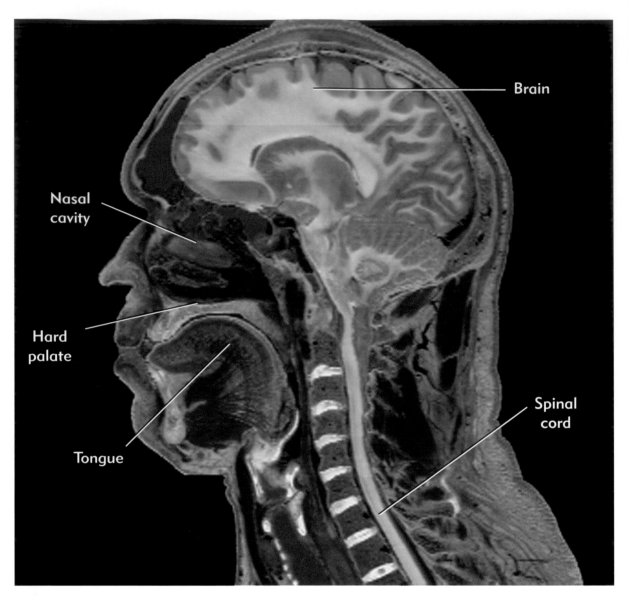

A cross-sectional view of the head showing the brain, nasal cavities, and mouth.

The ear serves another function that's every bit as important as hearing, and that's providing the body with its balance. Without the inner ear, it would be impossible for someone to even stand without falling over, let alone to walk or bend or turn. To easily test the truth of that statement, try twirling in circles until you are dizzy, then try to walk. In addition, the inner ear is responsible for coordinating eye movement, as well as eye and head movement.

It's the vestibular system within the inner ear that actually does the work. The three semicircular canals on the "head" of the "snail" deal with keeping the body stable when it turns. Whenever the body or head moves, the fluid in the semicircular canals moves as well, stirring like water in a pipe. As it moves, the fluid also stirs the tiny hair cells, the neural filaments that line the semicircular canals and are linked to the acoustic nerve. These neural hair cells signal to the brain that the body or head has moved.

Meanwhile, two tiny membranous sacs within the inner ear, the smaller saccule and the larger utricle, contain the same type of hair cells. In this case, they're disturbed only when the body moves forward or backward, stirred one way if it goes forward and the other way if it backs up. Then the hair cells signal to the brain that the body is moving and which way it's going.

There's one more amazing fact about balance and hearing. Not only are they both the result of the ear and the brain working in partnership, it's work of which we're not even aware.

3
HEARING DISORDERS

Wonderful though the ear is, any system that's so complicated and serves more than one function, as the ear does, can, and does, have things go wrong with it. A hearing disorder may be present from birth. In that case, it's called congenital. If it occurs after birth, the disorder is called acquired. Some doctors further subdivide acquired hearing disorders into prelingual (happening before a child learns to speak) and postlingual (happening after a child learns to speak).

Genetic problems are responsible for about half of all the cases of congenital hearing disorder. In fact, research into the human genome, the entire DNA "blueprint" of the human body, has revealed more than one "deafness gene" that may be responsible for hereditary deafness. Often, the problem comes from what is known as a recessive gene. Both biological parents may have perfectly normal hearing, yet they may carry a recessive "deafness gene" without realizing it. Their child would then have a 25 percent chance of inheriting both recessive "deafness genes" and being born with a hearing disorder. There are also some genetic syndromes that often include hearing problems, such as Down's syndrome or fetal alcohol syndrome.

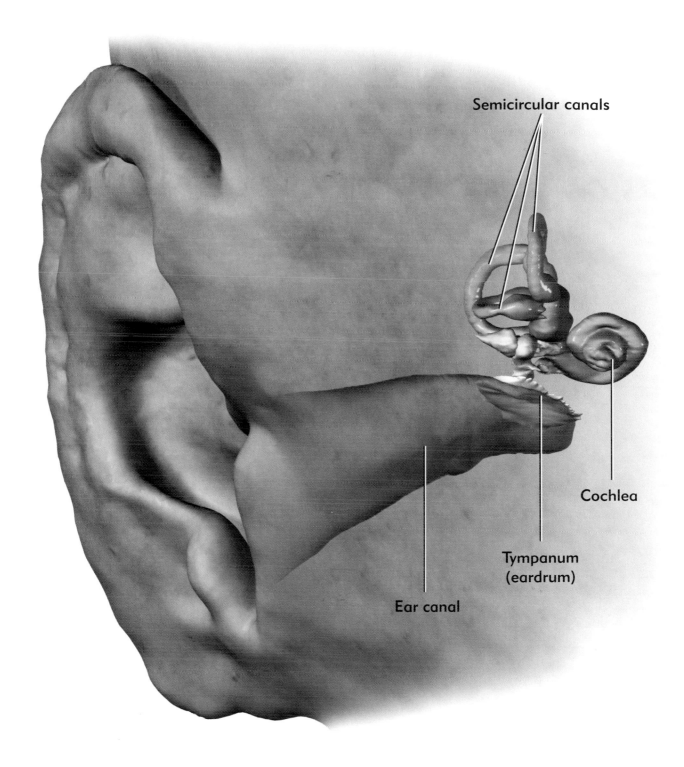

Semicircular canals

Cochlea

Tympanum
(eardrum)

Ear canal

The ear canal, eardrum, and semicircular canals lie just inside the ear.

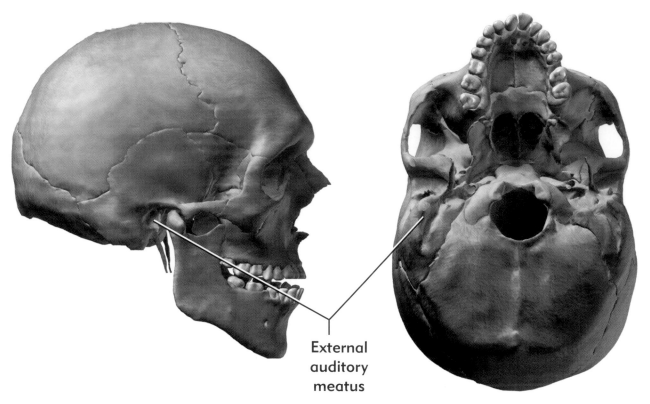

External
auditory
meatus

These two views of the skull show where the ear canal passes through the bone to the inner ear.

In addition, accidental exposure to harmful chemicals or environmental hazards can damage the genes of a developing embryo. Other problems include infections such as German measles, which can be passed to the embryo, and premature birth, which means that the ear structure may not have had a chance to develop properly.

Genetic deformation of the outer ear is called congenital microtia. The defect can range from something as minor as a missing fold of the helix, the edge of the outer ear, to a completely missing external ear. The shape of a malformed outer ear may block sound to the inner ear.

Congenital atresia means that there is no external ear canal. In these cases, a bony plate blocks the middle ear, often completely. What's worse is that congenital atresia is almost always accompanied by malformations of the middle ear bones as well. For instance, sometimes the malleus or the stapes are fused to other bones so that they can't move freely and transmit vibrations properly. In milder forms of atresia, the ear canal may exist but is much more narrow than normal, allowing less of the sound wave to enter the ear.

The second type of hearing disorder is called acquired hearing loss. This is generally not related to any genetic problems. Acquired hearing loss is something that can happen to someone at any stage of his or her life and has several possible causes, ranging from illness to injury.

The most common illness to affect the ear is called otitis media: the routine ear infection known to almost every child. Indeed, over 50 percent of children will have suffered an ear infection by the age of one. The reason for this is the fact that in children, the eustachian tube isn't as fully grown or slanted as it becomes in adults. This means that a child's ear is much more susceptible to infections. The middle ear becomes filled with fluid, and sound vibrations aren't passed along as efficiently. Sound becomes unclear or muffled. There can even be painful pressure put on the eardrum. Usually, the condition is temporary, and hearing clears up as soon as the infection is healed. But if ear infections are too common or too severe, they can damage the eardrum, or the bones and nerve. This causes a permanent hearing loss. Other diseases that can cause permanent damage to the inner and middle ear include measles, mumps, and meningitis.

In addition to diseases creating problems for the ear, cures for other, nonhearing-related diseases might also cause hearing harm. Some medicines, while perfectly harmless to hearing if used properly, become dangerous to the ear if they are used for long periods of time or taken in overly large doses. They can create enough fluid buildup in the inner and middle ear to cause permanent hearing loss. These medicines include very high doses of aspirin and some common antibiotics, including erythromycin and streptomycin.

Loss of Hearing

A teenaged girl who had attended a rock concert reported that a day later she still felt as though she had cotton in her ears, which were persistently ringing. It took several days for her hearing to completely return to normal. Former president Bill Clinton wears a small hearing aid to treat his minimal hearing loss, which is due, as he freely admits, to attending too many rock concerts in his teens.

What happened to the teen is called a temporary threshold shift, in which the hair cells of the cochlea malfunction but recover. Clinton wasn't so lucky. In his case, too many repeated episodes of such shifts caused a permanent threshold shift from which the hair cells couldn't recover.

A separate category of hearing problem is called tinnitus, which is a high-pitched and annoying ringing or buzzing sound inside the ear. Unfortunately, it has many possible causes, including exposure to loud noise, an ear infection, allergies, or seemingly no obvious reason at all. Sometimes tinnitus stops on its own, but sometimes it lasts long enough to badly interfere with sufferers' lives.

When tinnitus is accompanied by symptoms such as dizziness, nausea, and distorted hearing, it is called Meniere's disease. This disease involves the buildup of excessive fluid in the canals of the inner ear and is a common cause of hearing loss.

Yet another form of acquired hearing loss is called presbycusia, or age-related hearing loss. This condition begins with a loss of higher-frequency sounds, often while the person is in his or her forties, and gradually worsens over the years as the normal course of everyday life slowly wears down the hair cells of the cochlea. It's more common in men than women and possibly has a hereditary link.

Injuries form the second category of acquired hearing loss. Someone who has suffered a major head injury, such as the result of a car crash or too violent a tackle in football, may find that his or her injury includes damage to the ear, ranging from a ruptured, or torn, eardrum to fractures of the ear's bones. In addition, vigorous probing of the ear canal with a cotton swab or other object can puncture the eardrum, as can a panicky attempt to remove an insect. Far safer to let the insect leave by itself or to wash out the ear with warm water.

Sudden sharp, loud noises also do damage. People too close to exploding firecrackers or other explosions often suffer temporary hearing loss or, if they're unlucky enough to have an eardrum ruptured by the force of the blast, permanent hearing loss.

Being exposed to noise, including loud music, for a long time can also lead to hearing loss because the relentless sound wears down and destroys the cochlea's hair cells. This is a genuine problem for rock musicians, who often do suffer hearing loss. It's also a problem for anyone using headphones turned up too high, people whose hobbies include noisy vehicles such as motorcycles or snowmobiles, or those who work in a factory or on a construction job and don't wear protective earplugs. The real danger here is that someone may think he or she has finally gotten used to the noise and not realize that the reason is that he or she has suffered a hearing loss.

4

HEARING AIDS AND ADVANCES

Up to the end of the nineteenth century, people with hearing problems had few choices open to them. They could cup their hands under their ears to try to get more sound waves into the ear, or they could carry ear trumpets, which funneled amplified sound into the ear but literally looked like trumpets and were large, bulky, and not very effective. By the middle of the twentieth century, they could wear hearing aids, which were clumsy, noticeable, and not too efficient.

By the end of the twentieth century, all that had changed. Now, at the beginning of the twenty-first century, there are four different types of hearing aids: conventional, programmable, digital, and disposable.

The conventional hearing aid is the most basic type, not too far advanced from earlier designs except for being smaller and less noticeable. Conventional hearing aids are made up of a microphone, an amplifier, and a receiver. The wearer of a conventional hearing aid can change the device's volume, louder or softer, but that's all. Any major changes mean getting the device altered at the factory. And that means being without it for several days.

A programmable hearing aid is a definite step forward. It is set and adjusted by computer to match the wearer's needs. A programmable device usually has an automatic volume control as well, so that the

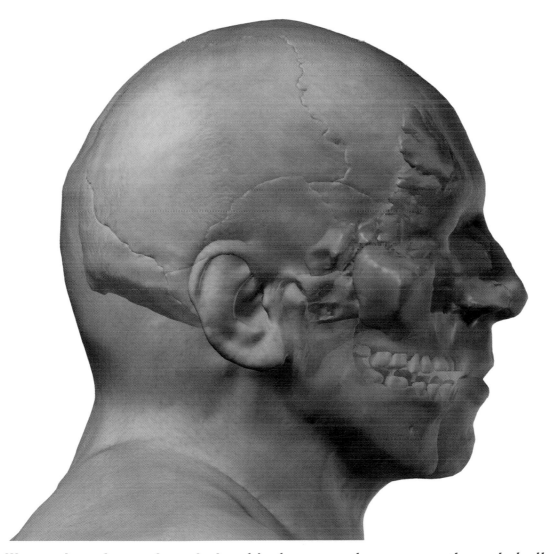

wearer doesn't need to worry about making adjustments. Any major changes can be made during a visit to the doctor's office.

The most modern version of the hearing aid is called the digital hearing aid. This is a totally new device that works with a computer chip that makes it programmable to very specific frequencies. It's called a digital hearing aid because it has a digital circuit that produces far clearer sound than the older hearing aids. It's still in the testing stage, but looks very promising.

This illustration shows the relationship between the ear, mouth, and skull.

The fourth type of hearing aid, the disposable device, is meant to be used for only a few months, or until a wearer's needs change, and then replaced. It isn't as sophisticated as the digital device.

There are also four different ways of wearing hearing aids. Completely-in-the-canal, or CIC, hearing aids fit neatly into the ear canal and are almost completely invisible. They aren't for anyone with the most severe hearing loss, or for children, whose ear canals are constantly growing with the rest of their bodies.

In-the-canal, or ITC, hearing aids are placed closer to the entrance of the ear canal and are more visible than CIC devices. In-the-ear, or ITE, hearing aids are placed at the entrance of the ear canal and are the most clearly visible. Behind-the-ear, or BTE, devices used to be fairly bulky and easily noticed. Modern technology has shrunk them, though they are still fairly noticeable. They can be dyed to match a user's natural skin tone.

Will scientists ever be able to completely repair damaged hearing? It seems more and more likely. There are already some successful surgical techniques that can repair damage wherever possible and even bypass damage that's too great to repair.

Congenital microtia, the lack of an outer ear, is obviously something that's noticeable at a child's birth. Usually, surgery is postponed until the child is four or five years old. By this age, the ear structure is more fully grown, but the child is still young enough to develop normal speech. The work is performed not by a doctor, but by a plastic surgeon working in conjunction with the doctor.

Until recently, the structure of the new ear was taken from the cartilage of one of the patient's ribs. But new advances in chemistry and cell growth are beginning to eliminate the need for a second surgery. Scientists are already able to grow skin and cartilage in the laboratory. Skin happens to be particularly easy to grow in sheets, and it is already

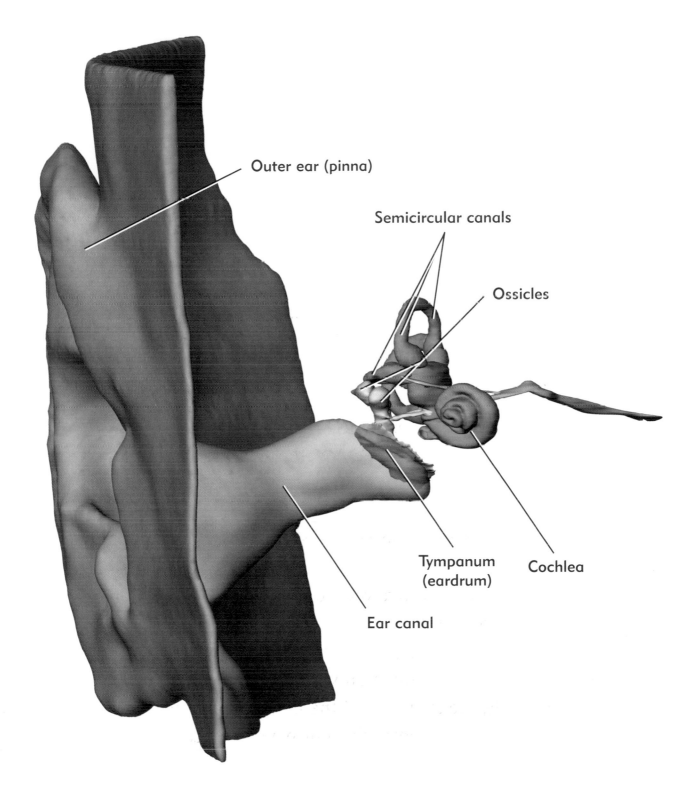

Outer ear (pinna)

Semicircular canals

Ossicles

Tympanum
(eardrum)

Cochlea

Ear canal

With the other parts of the skull and brain removed, the parts of the inner ear can be seen more clearly.

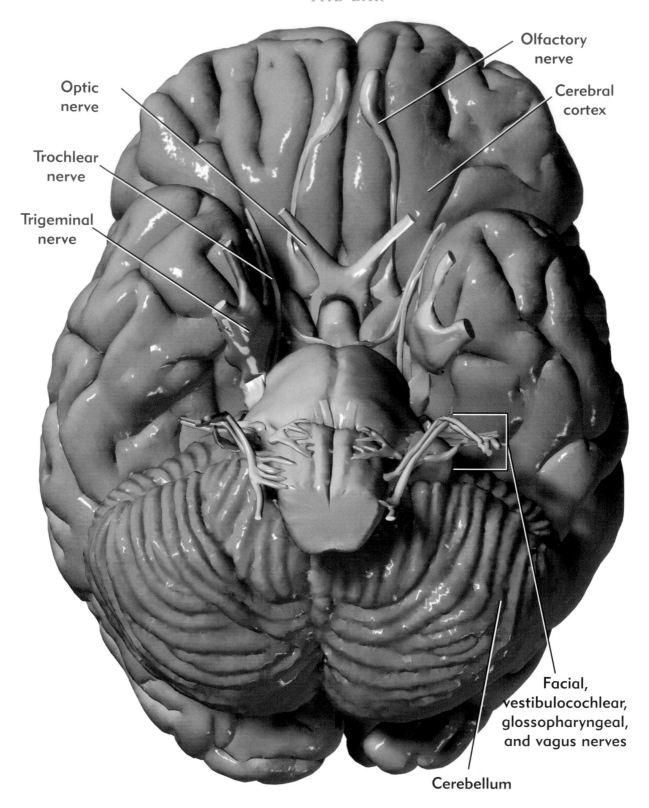

Olfactory
nerve

Cerebral
cortex

Optic
nerve

Trochlear
nerve

Trigeminal
nerve

Facial,
vestibulocochlear,
glossopharyngeal,
and vagus nerves

Cerebellum

The brain as seen from below. Various nerves from the sense organs enter the brain through its underside.

being used for skin grafts on burn victims. Since skin also grows swiftly, a few skin cells taken from a patient can be quickly grown into new sheets of skin that the victim's body won't reject.

In the process of building a new ear, a doctor would first take a few cells from the patient and grow them in a small sheet. The frame of the ear would be shaped out of laboratory-grown cartilage, also produced from the patient's cells, or from a polymer compound. "Polymer" is the term for a chain of molecules, such as polymer plastic. But our bodies produce polymer chains of molecules as well. The sheet of skin would be grown onto the ear framework. Then the new ear would be grafted onto the patient's head, giving him or her a brand-new, perfectly natural-looking ear.

The Ear and Outer Space

Since the beginning of manned spaceflight, there has been an increasing interest among scientists in the workings of the inner ear. How does it function in weightlessness? How can an astronaut adjust to the lack of gravity to give him or her a sense of balance? There's no up or down in space, after all. But astronauts discovered that they would instinctively decide for themselves which was the ceiling and which the floor of the space shuttle and the International Space Station. The problem comes when astronauts return to Earth. Then their inner ears have to learn how to balance their bodies once again. The process of readjustment usually takes a day or two. But it's important for scientists to figure out how to keep the inner ear functioning properly on longer space missions, such as those to Mars.

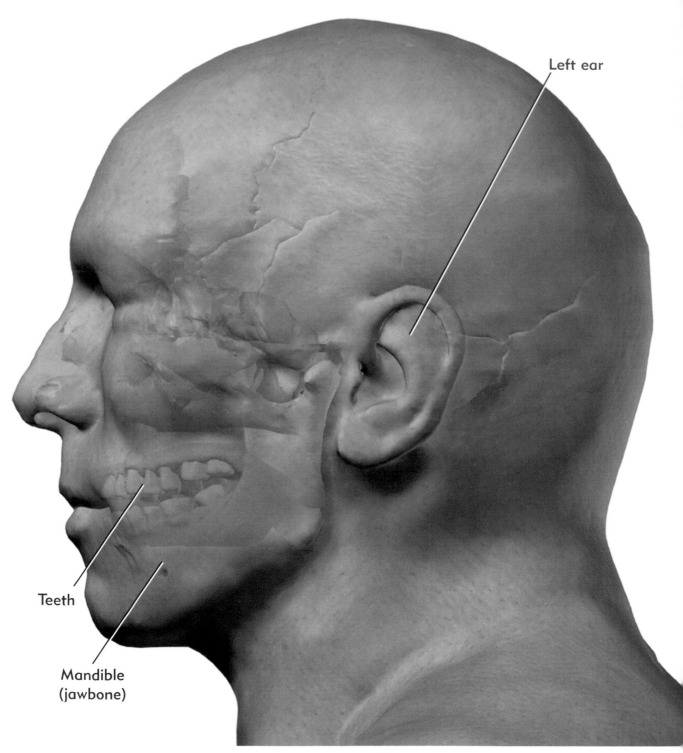

Left ear

Teeth

Mandible
(jawbone)

Externally, the ear has no moving parts. Ears on each side of the head enable us to determine which direction a sound is coming from.

The job of repairing the damage caused by congenital atresia, the lack of an ear canal, is more difficult. An outer ear can look perfectly normal, masking the trouble inside, and several states have begun ordering hearing tests for all babies. Examination of a child's ear through an accurate CAT scan tells the doctor the severity of the inner ear's damage. If it seems likely to the doctor that the child will be able to hear if surgery is performed, a difficult operation follows. The surgeon has to pick precisely the right spot to drill through the bone so that he or she can create a working ear canal. Since exposed bone is subject to infection, the surgeon also has to do very delicate skin grafts to cover the new canal. Sometimes it's necessary to reconstruct the middle ear as well, mostly to properly position the three bones. But it's worth all the effort if the surgery is successful because then the ear can hear normally.

Sometimes, though, the structure of the ear can't be repaired. In a new technique, cochlear implants can be surgically placed in the ear to bypass the damaged parts of the inner ear and directly activate the hearing nerve.

What will the future of the ear be like? Genetic problems such as hereditary deafness or congenital atresia will probably be eliminated within the century, or at least bypassed with much more sophisticated computerized hearing aids. It seems likely that within the century total deafness, which can't be helped with conventional hearing devices, will be eliminated as well.

But what about the ear itself and the range of human hearing? Will we someday be able to hear into the higher frequencies like a dog or even a bat? While the genetic engineering may be possible, the basic structure of our hearing doesn't seem likely to change too much. The ear is a pretty effective device, after all.

GLOSSARY

auricle   Entire outer ear, visible to the naked eye.

cartilage   Form of flexible connective tissue.

congenital atresia   Lacking an ear canal.

congenital microtia   Genetic deformation of the outer ear, ranging from minor to complete absence of the outer ear.

decibel   Unit of sound (loudness) measurement.

eustachian tube   Tube that connects the middle ear and the pharynx.

external auditory canal/external auditory meatus   Scientific names for the ear canal.

helix   Curve of the outer ear.

inner ear   Innermost part of the ear, containing the cochlea, which translates sound waves into signals to the brain, and the three semicircular canals that give the body its sense of balance.

middle ear   Section of the ear bounded by the tympanic membrane at one end and the inner ear at the other, and containing the ossicular chain.

ossicular chain   Three bones of the middle ear: the malleus, the incus, and the stapes.

otitis media   Scientific term for the common ear infection.

pinna   Bendable portion of the outer ear.

polymer   Chain of molecules.

tinnitus   Ringing or buzzing in the ear.

tympanic membrane   Thin membrane that vibrates when sound waves strike it; also called the eardrum

FOR MORE INFORMATION

Better Hearing Institute
515 King Street, Suite 420
Alexandria, VA 22314
(703) 684-3391
Web site: http://www.betterhearing.org

National Hearing Conservation Association
9101 East Kenyon Avenue, Suite 3000
Denver, CO 80237
(303) 224-9022
Web site: http://www.hearingconservation.org

SHHH: Self Help for Hard of Hearing People
7910 Woodmont Avenue, Suite 1200
Bethesda, MD 20814
(310) 657-2248
(310) 657-2249 TTY
Web site: http://www.shhh.org

Web Sites

HearingAidHelp.Com

http://www.hearingaidhelp.com

Hearing Loss Web

http://www.hearinglossweb.com

The Vestibular Disorders Association

http://www.vestibular.org

FOR FURTHER READING

Albee, Sarah. *What Do I Hear?* New York: Simon & Schuster, 1996.

Behar, Alberto, Marshall Chasin, and Margaret Cheesman. *Noise Control: A Primer*. San Diego, CA: Singular Publishing Group, 1999.

Hewitt, Sally. *Hearing Sounds*. New York: Children's Press, 1998.

Horowitz, Sue. *Hearing*. New York: The Rosen Publishing Group, Inc., 1996.

Northern, Jerry L. *Hearing Disorders*. Boston, MA: Allyn & Bacon, 1995.

Shimon, Debra A. *Coping with Hearing Loss and Hearing Aids*. San Diego, CA: Singular Publishing Group, 1992.

Tucker, Bonnie. *Cochlear Implants: A Handbook*. Jefferson, NC: McFarland & Company, 1998.

Turkington, Carol, and Allen E. Sussman. *The Encyclopedia of Deafness and Hearing Disorders*. New York: Facts on File, 2000.

Wilson, Merle A. *Your Sight and Hearing*. Rutland, VT: Health & Allied Science Publishers, 1996.

Yost, William. *Fundamentals of Hearing: An Introduction*. San Diego, CA: Academic Press, 2000.

INDEX

About the Author

Josepha Sherman is a professional author and folklorist, with over forty books and 125 short stories and articles in print. She's an active member of the Authors Guild and the Science Fiction Writers of America. Her Web site is at http://www.josephasherman.com.

Photo Credits

All digital images courtesy of Visible Productions by arrangement with Anatographica, LLC.

Series Design

Claudia Carlson

Layout

Tahara Hasan